# 300 PROGRESSIVE SIGHT READING EXERCISES FOR BASS GUITAR

**Volume 2**

**The primary goal of this book is to train the ability to read music and to free the musician from being dependent on tablatures or other communication systems that are not used in the academic or professional worlds. This book has been designed to train aural skills concurrently with reading skills.**

**Preview, instructions, video lessons and more:**

**www.RobertAnthonyPublishing.com**

**Instructional video links will be posted on this site as videos are produced.**

**If this book is helping you, please post a positive review at whichever website you had purchased it from. If you have requests, suggestions, or constructive criticism, feel free to use the email link on my website to let me know.**

**Free pdf downloads of manuscript, tab paper, keyboard and fretboard diagrams, and so on are available on my website.**

www.RobertAnthonyPublishing.com

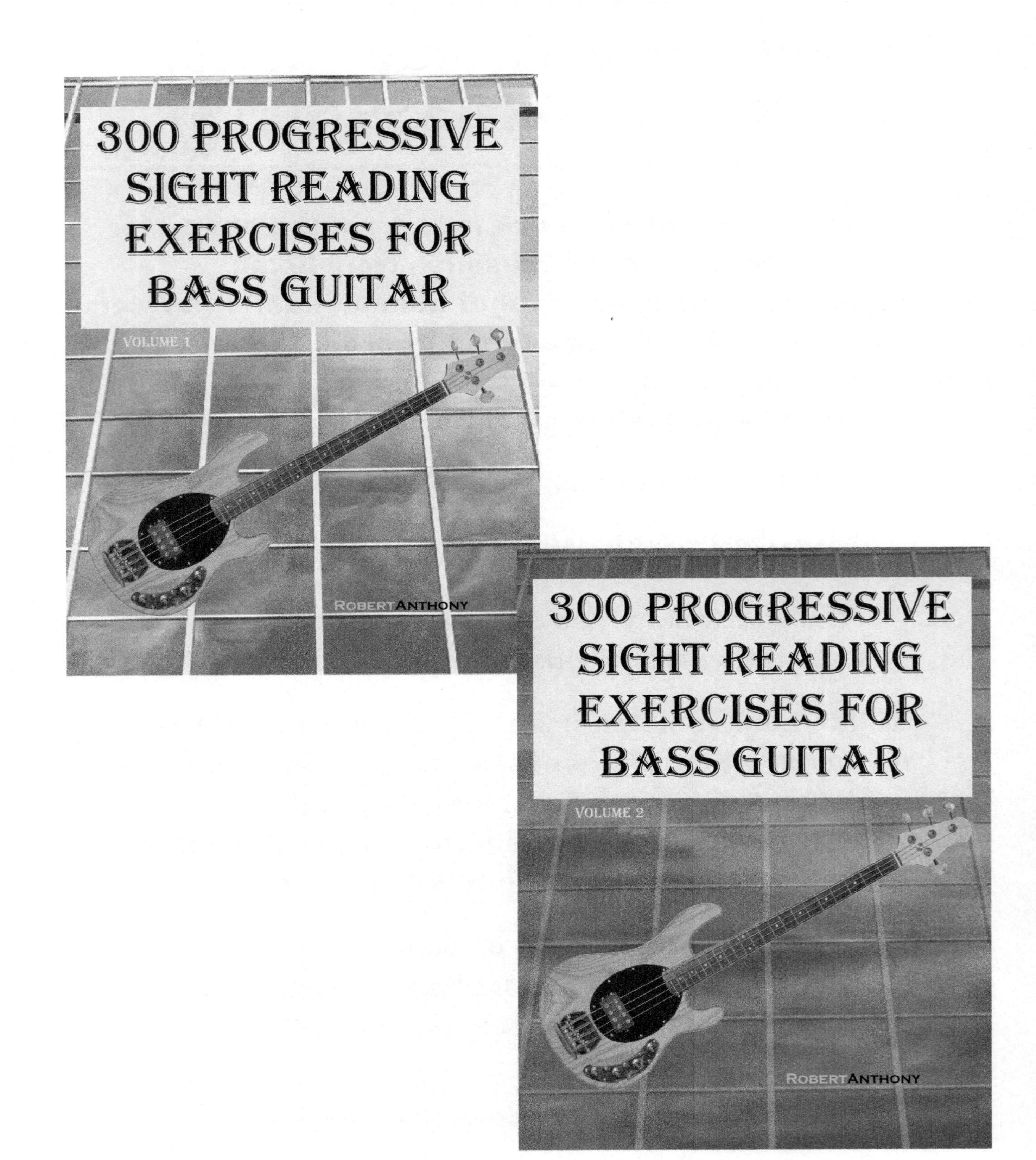

## Table of Contents

Foreword:

Volume Two starts out rhythmically simpler than Volume One ends, and then — of course — progresses to a more difficult level, adding dynamic markings, expanding the key signatures to C, G, F, D, Bb, A, Eb, E, Ab Major and their relative minor keys and modes, and adding the time signatures 3/8 and 9/8 into the mix.

Instructions and a free preview are available in pdf form at:
www.RobertAnthonyPublishing.com

Like in Volume One, the exercises are all eight measures (two phrases, or one period) in length. While they are composed to be melodic and pleasant to the ear, they are also composed to be difficult to memorize, and utilize many rhythms that seem to be absent from other sight reading books.

Next, I have made the staff font slightly larger than standard. While this will largely go unnoticed in the printed version of this book, it should make the electronic versions significantly easier to read.

Finally, there are many correct ways to use this book. The instructions and a preview in pdf form are posted on my website so that I can update the instructions as I discover additional strategies. For example, I sometimes receive emails in which people tell me how they like to use this book. My opinions will evolve the more I use this book to train my students, so I want the ability to easily update the instructions as needed. The link for the pdf download will be directly below the picture of the cover of this book. Instructional videos supporting this book will be posted, as they are created, in the same place.

~ Robert Anthony

# Major Scales

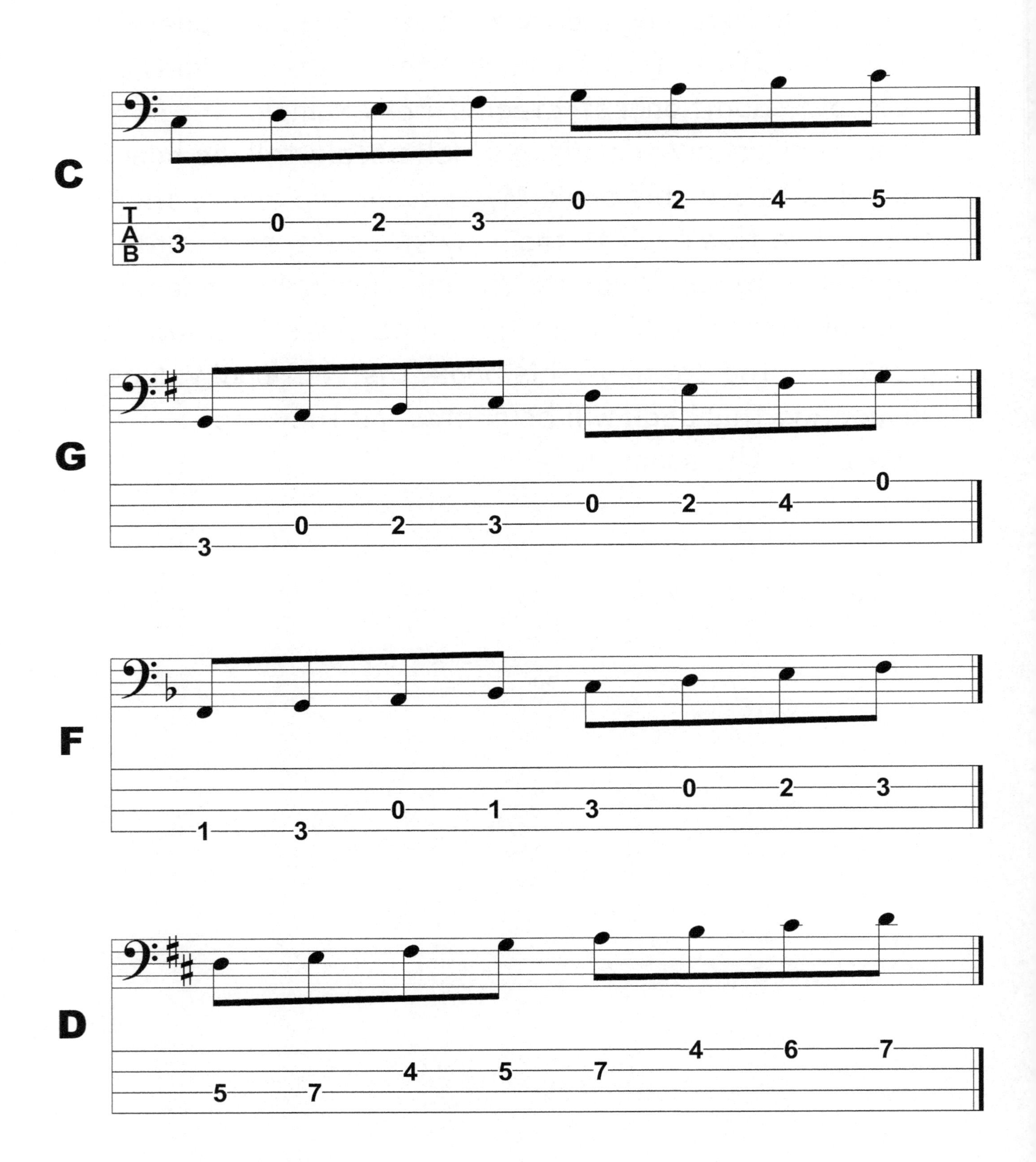

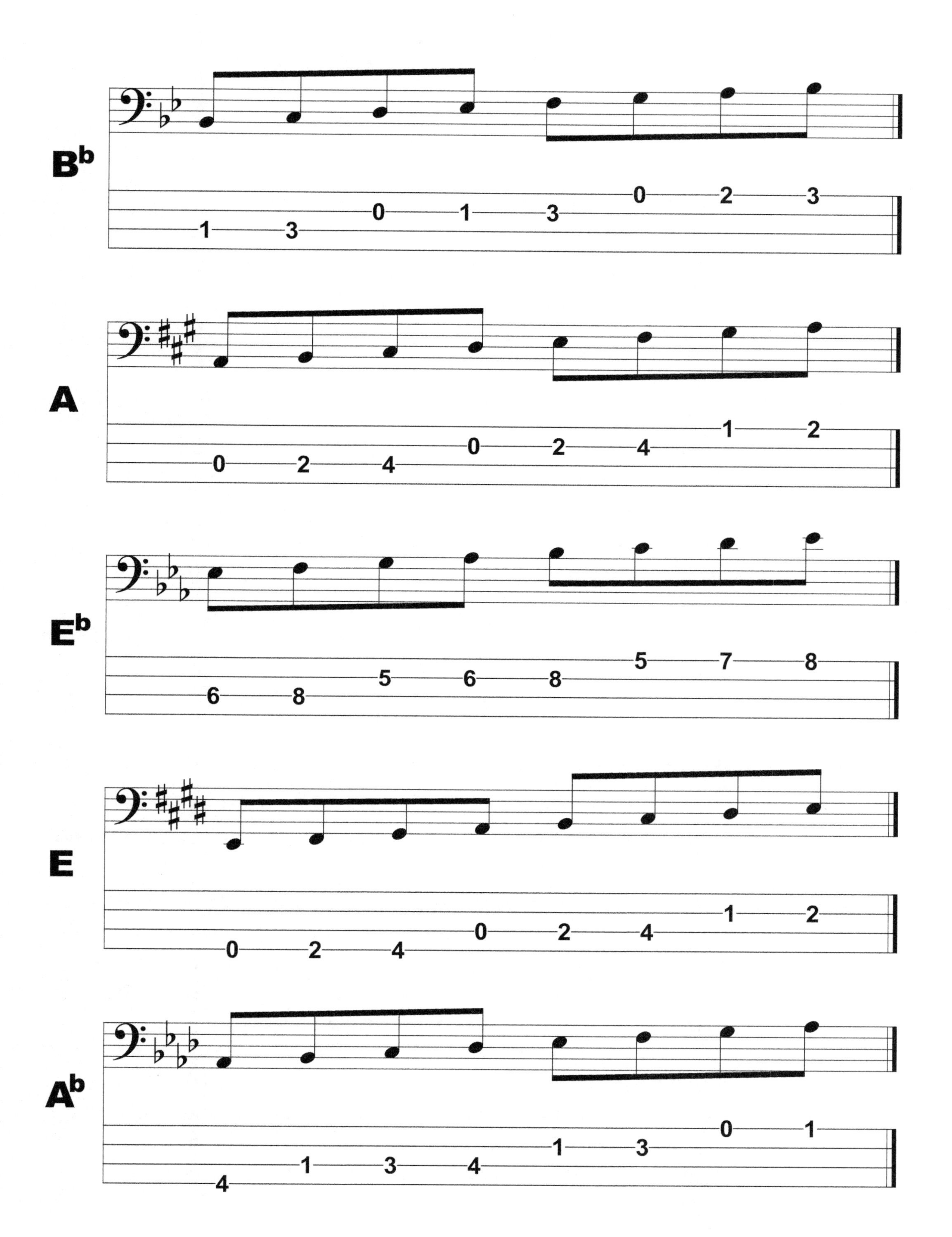
B♭
1 3 0 1 3 0 2 3
A
0 2 4 0 2 4 1 2
E♭
6 8 5 6 8 5 7 8
E
0 2 4 0 2 4 1 2
A♭
4 1 3 4 1 3 0 1

# Major Scales

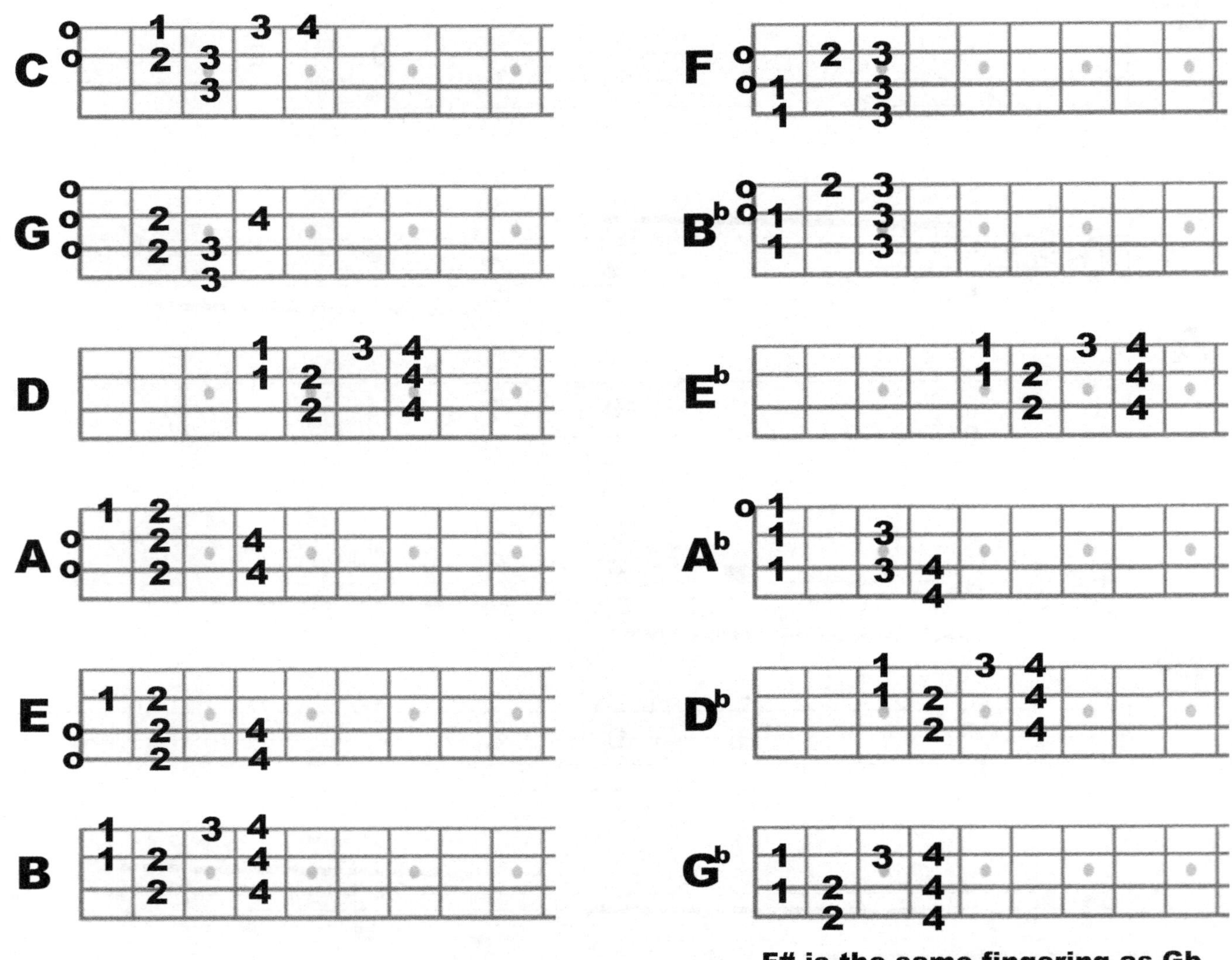


**F# is the same fingering as Gb**

**The twelve Major scale fingerings above are included for convenience. These will make memorizing the scales a much easier task. If you are uncertain how to read these, compare these to the the tablature versions (C, G, F, D, Bb, A, Eb, E, and Ab) that precede this page to help.**

**The Circle of Fifths on the next page will help to identify the key signature, and will let you know when to use which scale. Closed position (higher on the fretboard) scale fingerings will be included in the pdf instructions at: www.RobertAnthonyPublishing.com**

# Circle of Fifths

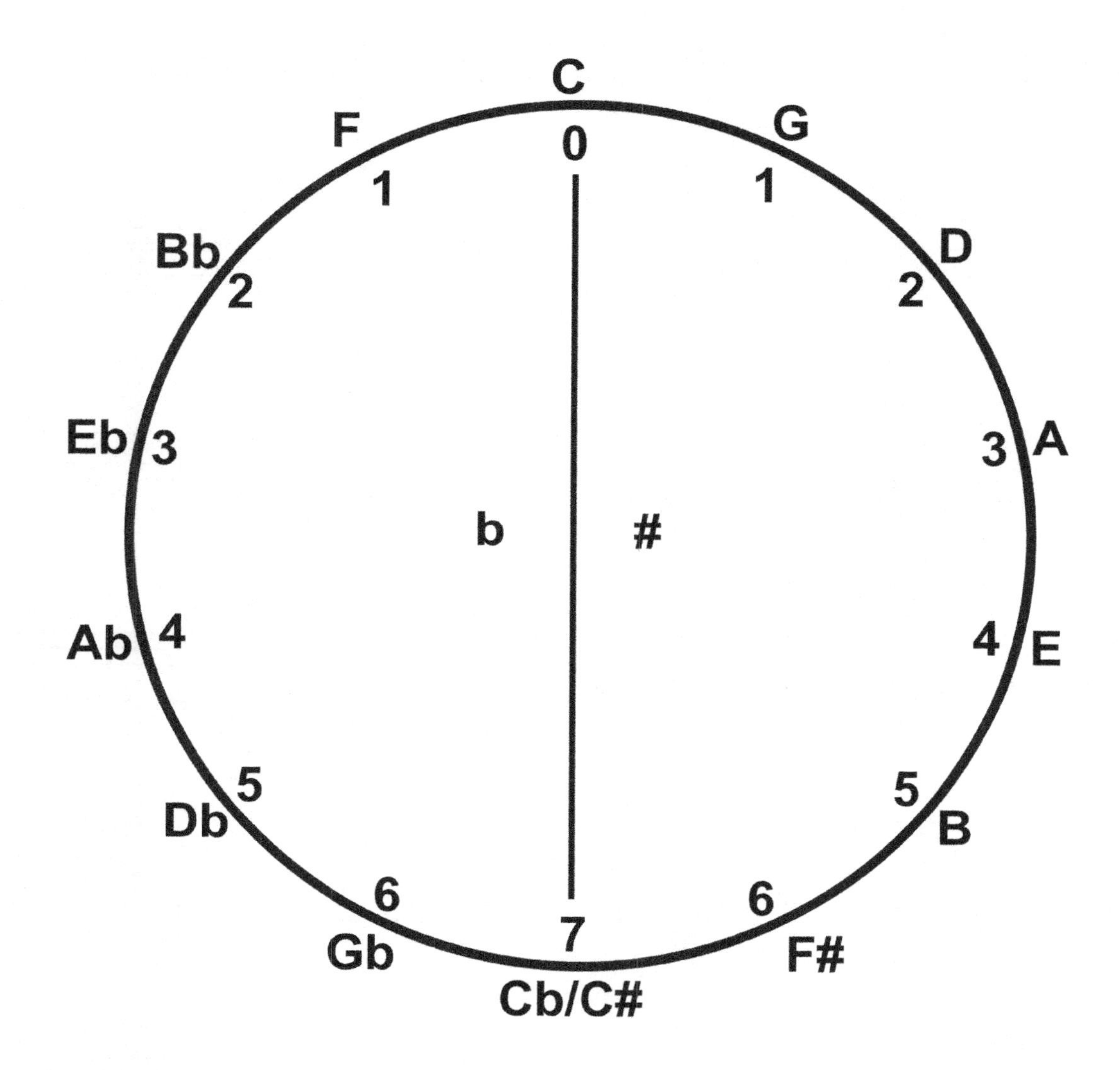


**You can use the Circle of Fifths to recognize key signatures by how many sharps (#) or flats (b) are in the key. The key of A Major has three sharps, for example, and the key of Bb has two flats. In the key signatures, sharps always occur in the order: F C G D A E B, while flats always occur in the opposite order: B E A D G C F. Level One uses only the keys of C (no sharps or flats) and G (All Fs are sharped). Sharps make a note one key higher, while flats make a note one key lower.**

**The following sentence will help you to memorize these orders:**

## Frank's Cat Got Drunk At Elmo's Bar

1
p
2
mp
3
mf
4
p

5
mp
6
mp
7
p
8
mf

9
f
10
mp
11
p
12
mf

13
p
14
mp
15
mf
16
f

17
f
18
p
19
mp
20
f

21
p
22
mp
23
mp
24
p

25
p
26
mp
27
p
28
mp

29
p
30
mp
31
mp
32
mf

33
mf
34
p
35
mp
36
p

37
p
38
mf
39
p
40
mp

41
mp
42
p
43
mf
44
f

45
p
46
p
47
mf
48
mp

49
p
50
mp
51
p
52
mf

53
mp
3
3
54
p
3
55
mf
56
p

57
mp
58
p
59
mp
60
p

61
mp
3
62
f
63
mp
3
64
p

65
f
66
mf
67
f
68
mp

69
p
70
mp
71
mp
72
mf

73
p
74
mf
75
f
76
mp

77
p
mf
78
mp
79
mf
80

81
p
82
mp
83
mp
84
mf

85
p
3
3
3
3
86
mp
87
mf
3
3
88
f

89
p
90
mf
91
f
92
p

93
mp
94
mf
3
95
f
96
mp
3

97
mf
98
mf
99
mp
f
100
p
mp

101
mf
mp
102
p
mp
103
mp
p
104
mp
mf

105
mp
mf
106
p
mf
107
mf
p
108
mp
f

109
p
mp
110
mp
3
p
111
mf
mp
p
112
f
3
3

113
p
f
114
mf
mp
115
p
mf
116
f
mf

117
mf
mp
mf
118
p
mp
119
mf
mp
120
p 3
3
mp 3

121
f
ff
122
mp
p
123
f
mp
124
mf
mp

125
mp
p
126
mp
mf
127
p
mp
128
mp
p
mp

129
p
mp
130
f
mf
131
p
mp
132
p
mp
mf
p

133
mf
mp
134
mf
f
135
mf
f
136
mp
mf

137
mf
mp
mf
f
138
p
mp
139
mp
mf
140
mf
mp

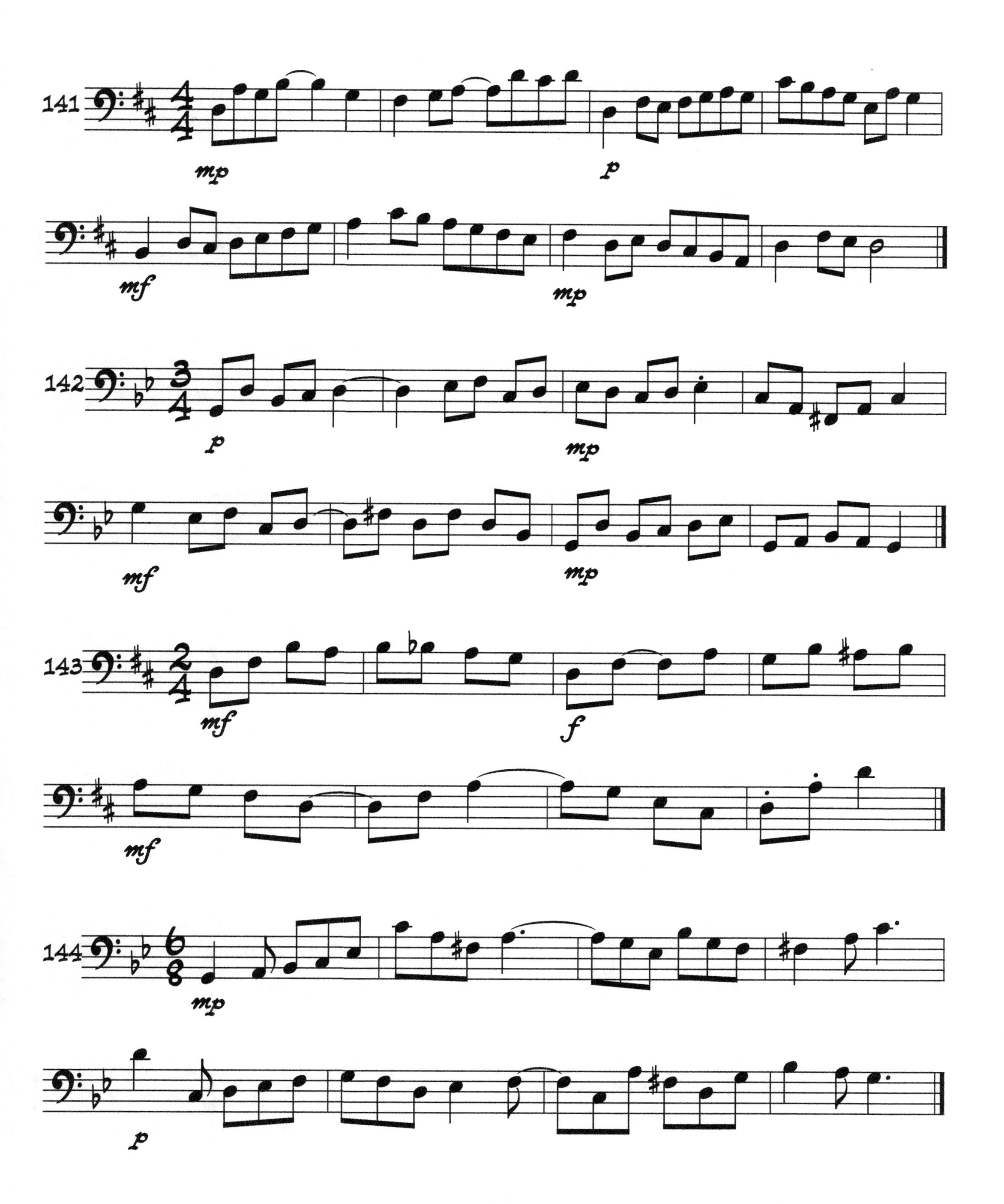
141
mp
p
mf
mp
142
p
mp
mf
mp
143
mf
f
mf
144
mp
p

145
p
mp
p
146
mf
f
147
p
mp
148
p
mp

149
mf
mp
p
150
mp
mf
mp
151
p
mp
p
152
mp
mf

153
mp
mf
154
mf
f
155
p
mp
156
mf
mp

157
mp
p
mp
158
mf
3
3
mp
mf
3
159
mp
mf
mp
mf
160
mf
f
mp
mf

161
mp
mf
162
p
mp
p
163
mp
mf
164
mp
p

165
p
mp
166
p
f
167
mp
p
168
p
mp

169
p
mp
170
mp
mf
mp
171
p
3
172
mp
p
mp
mf

173
p
174
mp
p
mp
175
mf
mp
3
176
p

177
p
mp
178
mp
p
179
p
mp
180
mp
p
mp

181
mp
mf
182
f
p
183
mp
mf
184
p
mp
p

185
mp
p
mp
186
mf
187
p
3
3
mp
188
mp
p

189
mf
mp
190
p
mp
f
191
mp
p
192
p

193
mp
f
mp
194
mp
195
mp
p
mp
p
196
mf
mp

197
mf
mp
mf
198
p
mp
p
199
mf
mp
200
mp
p
mp
mf
f

201
mp
f
mp
202
mf
f
203
p
mp
204
mf
mp

205
p
mp
206
mf
f
207
p
mp
208
mf
mp

209
p
mp
210
mp
211
mp
mf
mp
212
p

213
mp
p
214
mf
mp
215
p
mp
216
f
mf
mp
f

217
mp
p
mp
218
mp
mp
219
p
mp
p
220
p
mp

221
p
mp
mf
222
mp
p
mp
223
mp
3
p
3
mp
224
3
p
mp
3
3
p

225
mp
p
226
p
mp
mf
227
f
mf
f
228
mp
p

229
p
230
mp
mf
mp
p
231
mp
p
mp
232
p
mp

233
p
mp
mf
p
234
mf
p
f
235
p
mf
p
mf
236
mp
p

237
mp
mf
f
mf
238
mf
f
mp
p
239
mp
mf
p
240
p

241
p
mf
mp
p
3
242
mf
f
mp
243
3
p
3
mp
mf
244
mp 3
3
mf
mp 3
3

245
mp
246
p
pp
p
247
mp
248
p
mp
p
pp

249
mf
3
mp
3
mf
250
mf
mp
mf
251
mp
mf
mp
252
mf
f
mf

253
p
3
mp
3
254
mp
mf
f
255
p
mp
256
p
3
3
mp
3
mf
3
3
mp

257
p
258
p
pp
3
p
3
259
f
260
mp
mf
p

261
mf
262
mp
3
263
p
mp
p
pp
3
264
f

265
p
mp
mf
266
mf
3
mp
p
3
mp
267
f 3
mf
mp 3
f
268
mf
mp
p

269
mp
mp
3
270
mf
mp
p
271
mp
3
mf
3
272
p
mp
mf

273
p
mp
mf
mp
274
p
mp
p
pp
275
mp
mf
f
mp
276
p
p
mp

277
mf
mp
mf
278
mp
mf
279
mp
p
mp
280
mp
mf
mp

281
mf
mp
mf
282
mf
3
mp
f
283
mp
p
mp
mf
284
mf
3
mp
3
mp

285
mp 3
p 3
mp
286
mp
287
f
288
p
mp
p

289
mp
p
mp
mf
290
mp
3
3
3
291
p
mp
292
mf
3

293
mf
294
p
295
p
mp
mf
296
mp
p
pp

297
mf
mp
298
3
p
3
3
3
299
f
300
mp
3
p 3

www.RobertAnthonyPublishing.com

## Glossary of Musical Terms

**Adagio**: slowly
**Allegretto**: fairly fast
**Allegro**: fast
**Andante**: moderately slow
**Andantino**: usually faster than andante
**Animato**: lively, animated
**Cantabile**: in a singing style
**D.C. al Fine**: repeat from the beginning until fine
**Dolce**: sweetly
**Expressivo**: expressively
**FIne**: the end
**Grave**: very slow, solemnly
**Grazioso**: gracefully
**Lento**: very slow
**Mesto**: sad
**Moderato**: Medium Tempo
**Ritard**: slow down
**Très Expressif**: very expressive
**Vivace**: lively
**Waltz**: in three

## Dynamic Markings

**Pianissimo ~ pp**: very softy
**Piano ~ p**: softly
**Mezzo Piano ~ mp**: moderately soft
**Mezzo Forte ~ mf**: moderately loud
**Forte ~ f**: loud
**Fortissimo ~ ff**: very loud

# Identifying Note Names in Bass Clef

## Traditional Approach

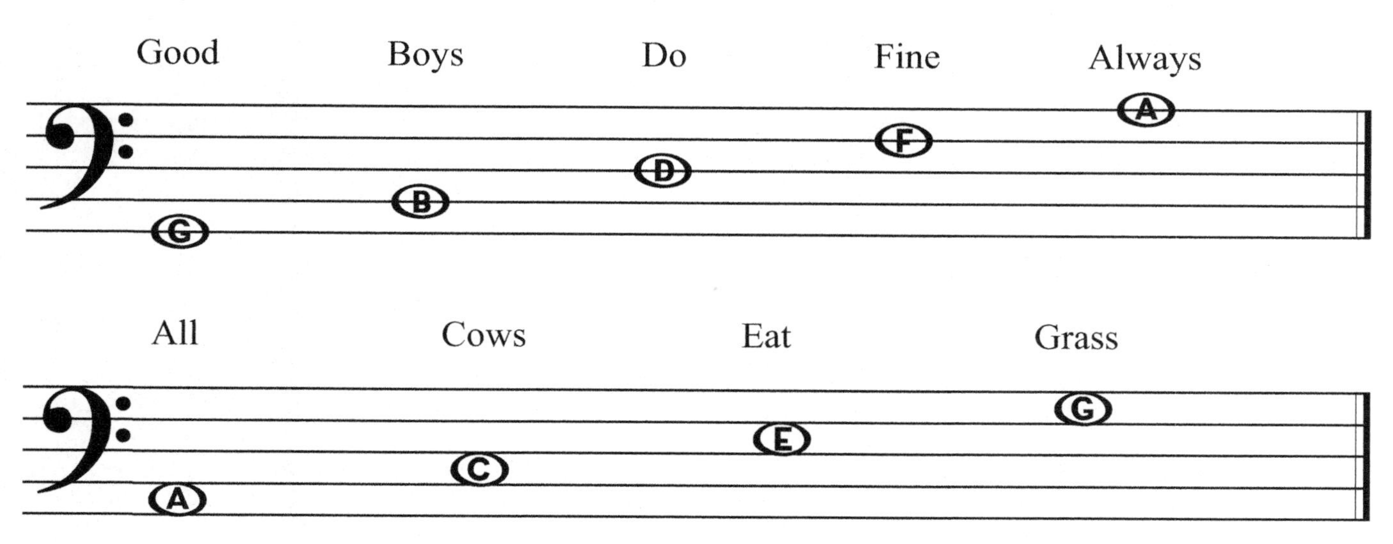


While the traditional approach above is helpful, you will likely find it to be easier to be aware that the musical alphabet (ABCDEFG) simply ascends the lines and spaces of the staff.

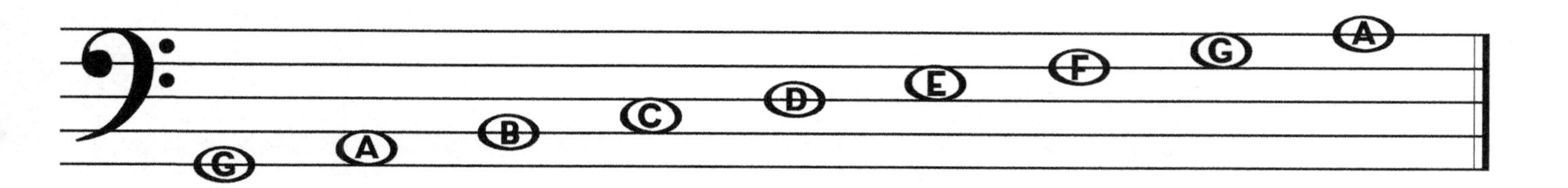


Ledger lines are used to extend the range of the staff as pictured here:

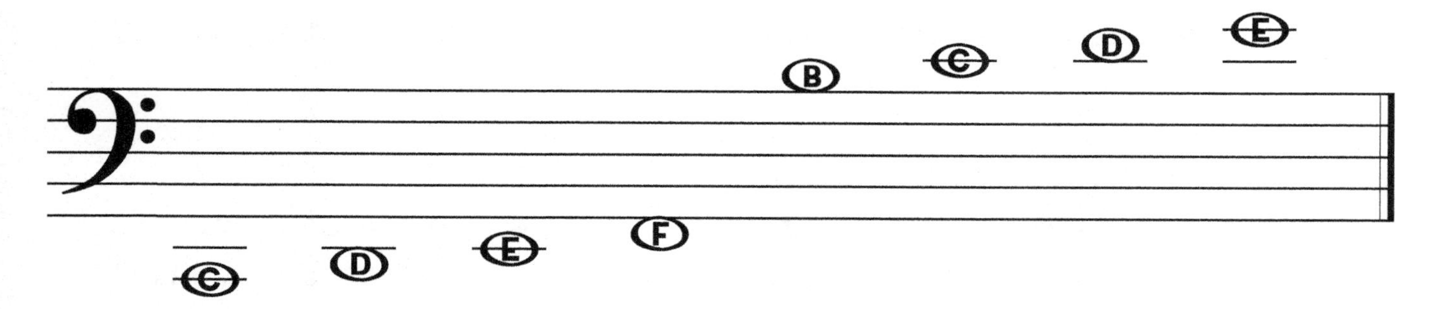

# Counting Rhythms in 4/4

# Counting Rhythms in 3/4

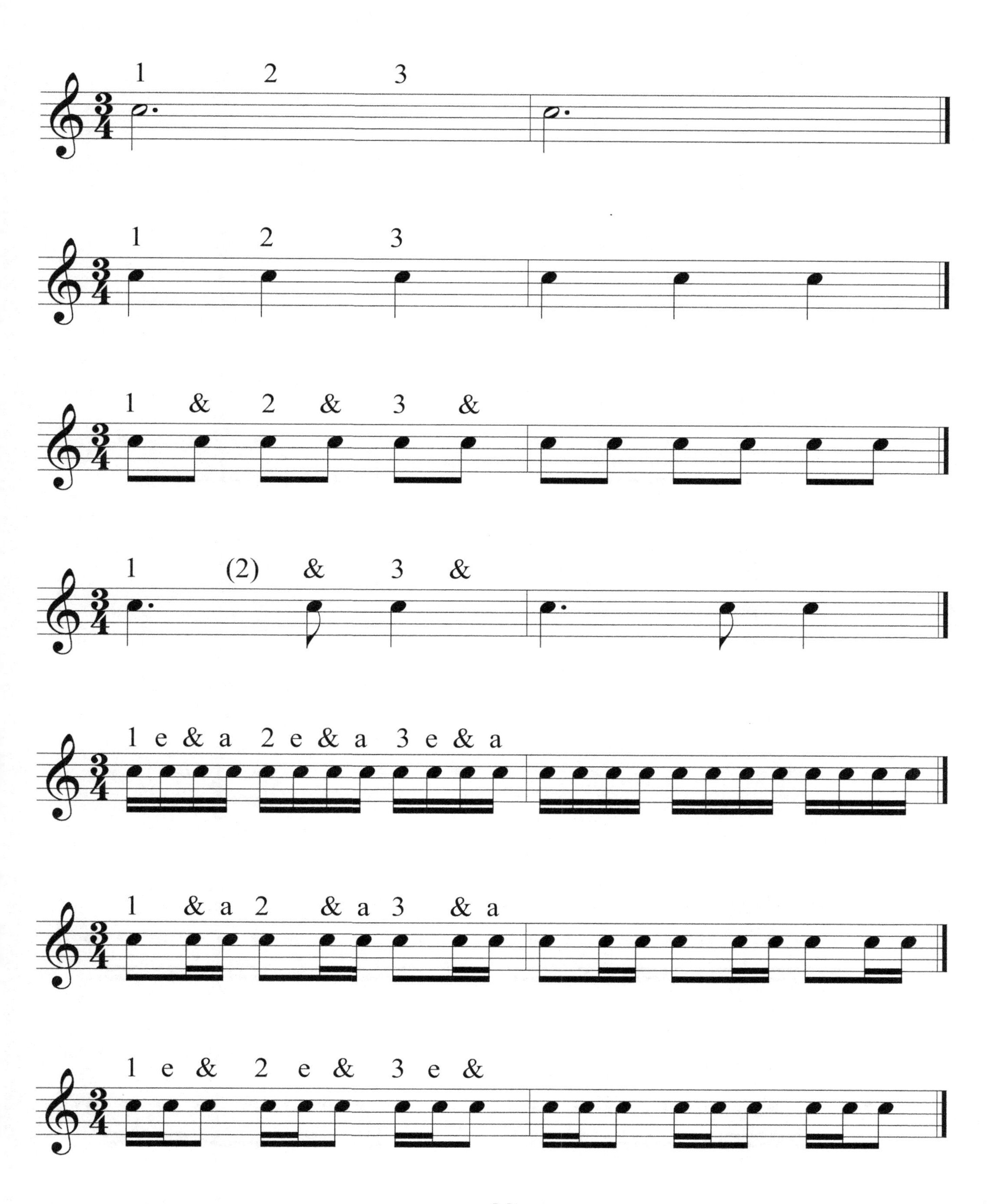

# Counting Rhythms in 6/8

# Counting Rhythms in 3/8

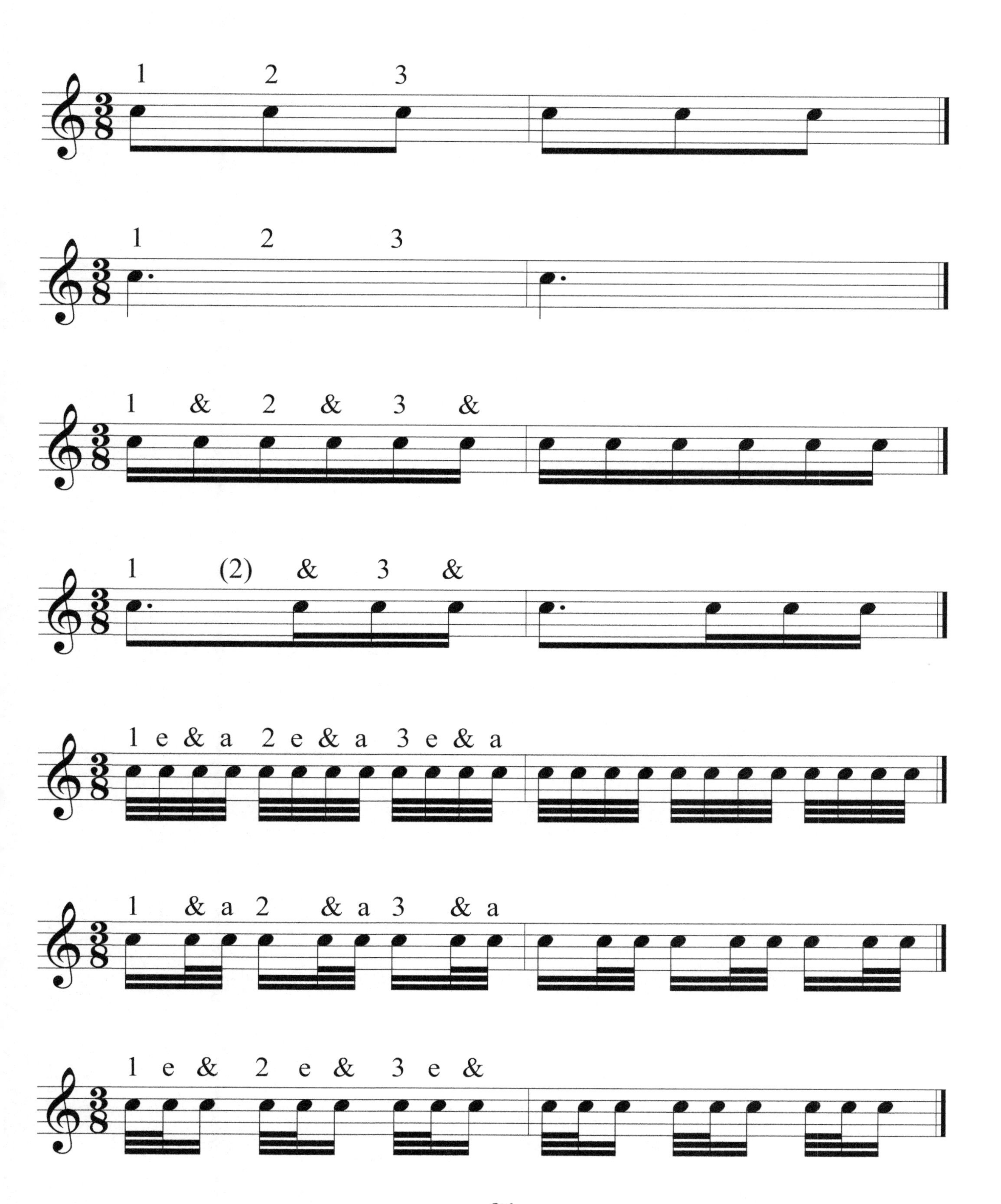

Free pdf download available at:
www.RobertAnthonyPublishing.com

T
A
B

T
A
B

T
A
B

T
A
B

T
A
B

T
A
B

T
A
B

T
A
B

**Free pdf download available at:**
**www.RobertAnthonyPublishing.com**

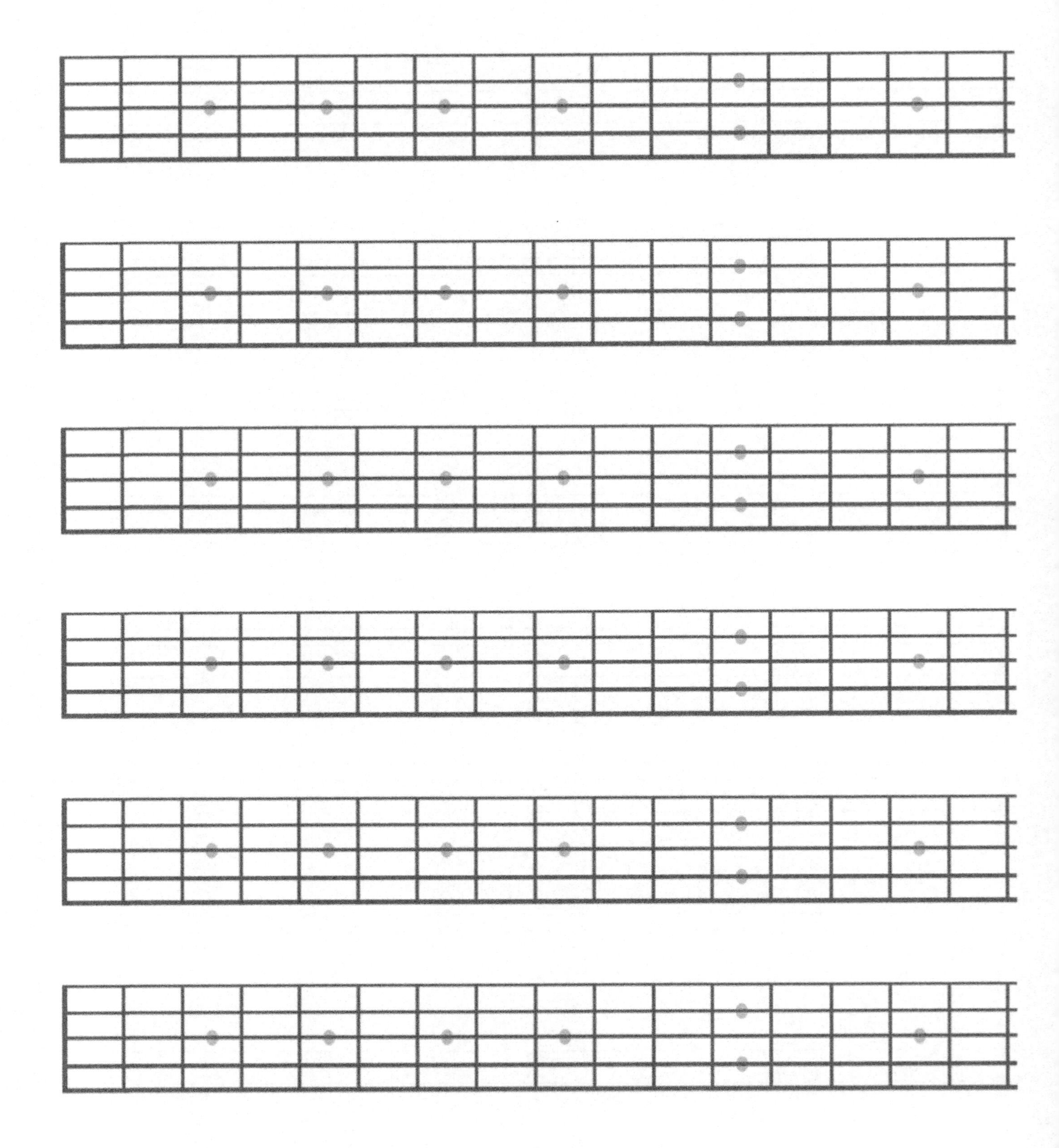

www.RobertAnthonyPublishing.com

Printed in Great Britain
by Amazon

37469873R00057